THE TALES OF A SLEEPY MIND-BOOK 01- REACHES A LAND OF TREASURE

R.Ishudh Abhinawa

Chennai • Bangalore

CLEVER FOX PUBLISHING
Chennai, India

Published by CLEVER FOX PUBLISHING 2024
Copyright © R.Ishudh Abhinawa 2024

All Rights Reserved.
ISBN: 978-93-56487-71-0

This book has been published with all reasonable efforts taken to make the material error-free after the consent of the author. No part of this book shall be used, reproduced in any manner whatsoever without written permission from the author, except in the case of brief quotations embodied in critical articles and reviews.

The Author of this book is solely responsible and liable for its content including but not limited to the views, representations, descriptions, statements, information, opinions and references ["Content"]. The Content of this book shall not constitute or be construed or deemed to reflect the opinion or expression of the Publisher or Editor. Neither the Publisher nor Editor endorse or approve the Content of this book or guarantee the reliability, accuracy or completeness of the Content published herein and do not make any representations or warranties of any kind, express or implied, including but not limited to the implied warranties of merchantability, fitness for a particular purpose. The Publisher and Editor shall not be liable whatsoever for any errors, omissions, whether such errors or omissions result from negligence, accident, or any other cause or claims for loss or damages of any kind, including without limitation, indirect or consequential loss or damage arising out of use, inability to use, or about the reliability, accuracy or sufficiency of the information contained in this book.

Greetings!

First of all I would like to thank the people who actually helped me write this incredible journey. There isn't much but they are of great importance.
My laptop, My parents, Imran Uncle from the computer store at Unity Plaza, and My Best Friend!
The above people supported me, encouraged me and provided me with all that I needed!
The story is of a boy who dreams of love to escape reality and there lies a deeper meaning within....

Thank you,
Ishudh Abhinawa

"Dreams of sleep shall bring tales of joy, they might bring your loved ones back, but they never shall be reality unless one makes it so, it is the ultimate bitter truth.."

-R.Ishudh Abhinawa
A Dreaming Child

I dedicate this to myself

-CHAPTERS OF THE BOOK-

01) LET'S GET TO KNOW THESE ONES
8-9

02) A CONVERSATION
10-13

03) HOW DO I GET BACK?
14-22

04) I THINK THERE'S A WAY
23-26

05) WHAT? IT IS?
27-30

06) THE DAY HAS COME...
31-33

07) THE GREAT REQUEST
34-39

08) ALL IS SET!
40-42

09) A BIG MISSION OF DREAM STARTS
43-47

10) PREPARE OF BATTLE
48-51

11) LET THE BATTLE BEGIN
52-58

12) REACHES A LAND OF TREASURE
59-64

13) A PUZZLE OF LOVE
65-68

14) THE ENDING IS ALWAYS HAPPY AND SHORT
69-70

CHAPTER 01
LET'S GET TO KNOW THESE ONES!

The morning sun takes a bright spot right at the edge of the sea. "It's the far end and end of all!" continued Ruddey, father of 1. That one was Tones, he was 6 at the time and had a mind more fresh than of a newly plucked and spot on ripen apple.
"Is it really the end, dad?" asked Tones in tone of a high pitched guitar. "Hoho, that's what they say now, no one to cross the waters, alright, it's home to

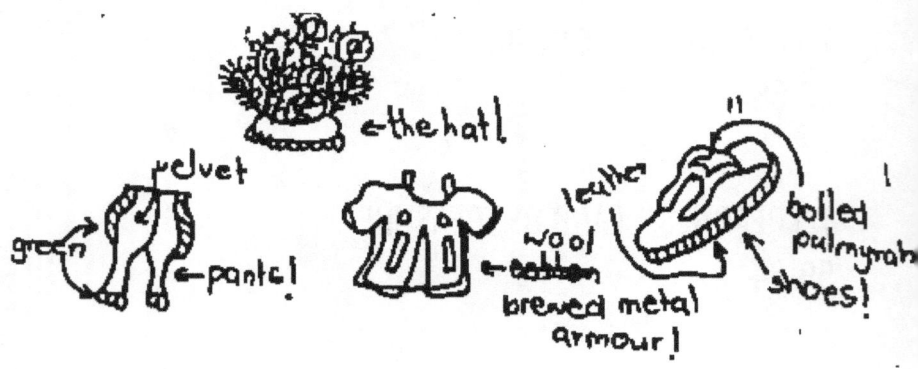

Yeld!"replied Rud, short for Ruddey. We will use Rud from now on.

You see, Rud and Tones were Domics, they wore pants of green and velvet, puffed at the thighs and wool brewed armours of strong metal. The outfit was really confusing! They even wore hats of Peacock feathers, well, some of them that is. And even shoes! Made of thick leather sewed onto leaves of boiled Palmyrah!.

These people lived in the times when Earth was not at all like now! They were the most ancient kind of people.

It is said, that they lived as power back in those days till something befell...(according to them)

Domics believed of the edge of the planet being the end point of imagination, they didn't know ships at all, the Earth was one and the waves covered the rest. They named the seas, Yeld! And the earth Drong!

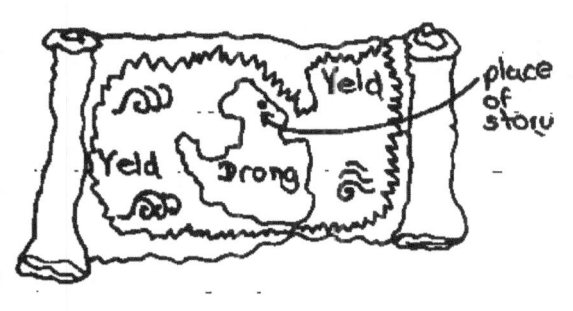

So far the Domics had spread out in the North Easts of Drong. Now let's zoom in back to the town of Nebulus, the main city of Drong and the Domics. This is where Ruddey and Tones live.

CHAPTER 02
A CONVERSATION

"Yeld, What's that?" asked little Tones as he pointed his index as to show the vast expanse of the crystal-shiny blanket of blue wrinkles. "Yeld, well, sonny.

That is the home of the others, like us, deep down lives the Yeldians hence the word Yeld of course!"

The sun was fresh yet at the same spot in the bright light blue sky.

"Come on now! Dad, Go on! How did it all start?"
"Oh Alright then, here goes..." started Rud with a nice exhale, signifying the start of a long tale...
"You see, our ancestors have said Drong wasn't like this,

not even Yeld! Everything was at rule by fire! Hot, burning liquid! Not sure what it was called though, maybe something called lav—a—aa— but anyways! It all cooled down eh, and all was tough as a rock because it was rock after all!

The air was still warm as fire though, hmm..... A few flings later however, everything was chill and beneath a few rocks erupted Yoda, Goddess to Drong and Yeld! She flew across the dusty and warm sky and muttered a set of words that you and I, my child are of reason to... "Drenga to Yolda " she muttered and BAM! A huge part of the land of rock was now lush of green and life and it was named Drong while the rest was conquered by waves and was named Yeld! Our home Nebulus, the city of Drong.. It all dates back here!" Rud now unfolded his hand onto the Village of Nebulus in face of courage and pride.

the → peacock

the sheep

cattle

"Oh I know that's not it! How did we form?! And who came first, the creatures?" Tones asked enthusiastically as his eyebrows now bent upwards as a rainbow emphasising his extreme desire to know more!

"Yoda wanted some company, you know, so she created her most favourite animal, the peacock! It is from them that we get the stuff for our hats alright! And well after that Yoda created these white woolly fellas, the sheeps, and well after that the cattle! OOH! And the sheep is where we get the wool for the wool broth and the cattle? Well, it's for the leather soles!" replied Rud not losing a drop of his excitement during the conversation.

"And us?"

"Well, that's a question you ask yourself dear…"

Little Tones was seriously confused, you could tell as his joyous filled eyes now crippled back inwards to his skull and his eyelids narrowed as his mouth showed an expression of suspicion.

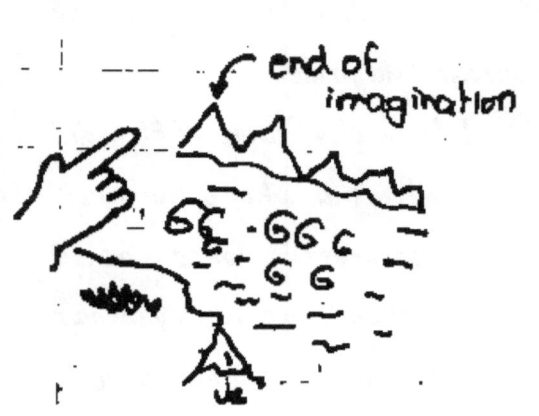

"What do you mean 'ask myself dad' !?" Tones finally expressed himself after a minute of utter confusion.

"Well, it means, you'll find it out one day," continued Rud, pointing his index towards the edge of horizon of the sea, where the sun, which was once there some time ago had risen up towards the high sky, Rud went on, "There, if your mind crosses that field of imagination, the end point of it, you'll find the true meaning of all this, many, many had tried but failed to do so..."

"Well if there's anyone that could do it, that would be me, definitely!" rang Tones quite fiercely considering the fact that he was in completely the opposite mood a few minutes ago...

"HO HO, it's not as easy as you think, you must be able to harness the power of consciousness and dream to conquer the end point!" replied Rud as if lecturing a university student.

Tones was quite un-surprisingly dumbfounded at this statement but proceeded to stare at 'the end point of imagination' with not any questions at all...

CHAPTER 03
HOW DO I GET BACK?

"TR–TR–INNN–GG" rang Tones's alarm bell. It was none-other than the time to wake up for school. Tones, unlike the other common mornings, was quite frantic this day. He got up quite quickly and ran his fingers from head to toes in motion of surprise and confusion.

"What was I WEARING?" he asked himself. Tones had indeed seen a dream, unlike any of the others. He forgot most of it and only seemed to find bits of memory about the dream in his mind.

"Hmm. whatever" he self talked back again as he rubbed his dry eyes and dropped his feet on to the floor. He zoomed back into his mood of 'sleep' again as he walked across the room, which had walls of dark green and carvings of mountains and a bed and another bed beside it, a cupboard next to the bed, a computer desk and a window that displayed his neighbours back yard for some reason.

"Tones! Come on now!" cried his Mum, Natalia, she was arrogant, deadly, ferocious, cunning, and all the words used to describe a completely evil person can be used on her, no questions asked.

She was a very thin, wine bottle structured woman who showed no mercy upon any kid let alone Tones. "Coming  alright, brushing my teeth!" replied Tones in a very...very...very... hateful manner, quite obvious as to why he said so actually.

She was the kind of mother to serve her kid pasta whilst killing him mentally(fortunately). Tones had already brushed his teeth and washed his face, now, he was heading down to have his morning breakfast which, as you guessed, is highly uncooked pasta.

"It's fish pasta, I don't care if you hate it but you better be shoving it down with no complaints or I SHALL!" raged Natalia, it was more of a rap tone to be quite honest. "Well, in that case, you know... nevermind..." replied Tones in an extremely disgusted manner.

As he sat on the wooden chair right near the dine table, he having not anything at all to think about, scavenged the room with his 2 marble blue eyes as if a predator was to catch its prey.

The rusty old fridge served some interest to being looked at as it was breaking down, live in motion. The sink with dirty plates was smelly as it was yesterday. There, right next to the sink laid his pasta...

"Boy, get your buttocks off the chair, whatever you're looking at, get the food yourself, it ain't going to walk towards you!" alarmed Natalia as if an alarm set to be rung as eyes were to observe her immensely raw pasta.

Tones was to get his pasta, now, but suddenly his brain was flushed with more memories, memories of his dream. Till that point he just remembered his abnormal suit or just the fact he was wearing something but now he remembered the scene. The setting of Drong itself.

"Nebulus, East of Drong!" he whispered to himself, knowing if he ever did shout, it would quite not be normal but highly psychotic.

He was decoding on how the building of the town looked like. Oh, and this would be the perfect time to give a description on how the building of the town of Nebulus did actually look like. It was not at all human, much more like a copy and paste. Each house had its own common owner. A herdsman would have

a cattle house and so did all of the other herdsmen in Nebulus. The house has a lengthy rod shaped structure, indicating the 4 legs of the cow and where's the head you might ask? Well, these herdsmen kill the cows for leather by slaying off their heads and so no head! They even have an outside shed-like part for selling their products, mainly being cattle leather

sandals and these people were found to be in Palmyrah tree businesses as well and meat as well... Then there is the Peakers house, it was where ,obviously, the people who sell peacock feathers and products live at. The houses normally had a large statue of a peacock built of carved out granite, and on either side of the main house lay 2 sub small houses, these were the places where the peakers kept their storage items at but is mainly built to resemble the 2 wings of a peacock in action! The 2 stone carved peacock feathers built in between the main and 2 sub houses are just there for aesthetics.

Then we got the Shepters House, they handle sheep wool and sell it, they even extract metal to make those wool brewed armours! The houses have woolly roofs and on the right there laid the metal extraction point while on the left laid the wool making and selling point. The, the people who had no main job at all, and engaged in other small, minor jobs had houses with stone

slabbed roofs and redstone walls with 2 electrone plants on either side, the plants were a symbol of good luck(according to the Domics that is.... It was overall an average town and Tones remembered the layout of the town most precisely, the cliff side edged to the vast ocean and all others...

Tones had finished eating now.

"Alright, I'm done, it was filthy as ever!" yelled Tones.
"You better be grateful you little brat for I am keeping you alive when your father's dead!" replied Natalia as if a snake were to hiss during a commencing of a fight with a mongoose.

"Dad...Dad! Was there! With me!" Tones was a bit emotional now that the 'father' topic was brought up. "My dad was with me in my dream!" Tones was now rescanning his memories back again to try and mine out more information where he was quite successful. Tones's school was Midst Highway College, the school was near, fortunately, a couple of metres of a walk through Drouters route was it located.

All the time, Tones had to walk there as his most grateful mother didn't seem to suffice Tones with his needs of transportation.

The walk was not bad at all, it was his stomach which was rumbling like a magnitude 4.5 earthquake. Soon, however, he had much more things to worry about as he, now, had reached school.

As all Tones had his own personal bully who bullied him free of charge, however he was not at all physically abusive but rather mentally and he really doesn't try to snipe Tones down every time but it is quite often. The bully's name was Trotter, quite a name eh? Midst Highway College was big, having a ton of space to roam, which means a ton of space in which a bully can get to you with no risk of him getting into trouble at all!

Tones was in danger zone, he was passing along the locker room of chatter and extreme crowd, the kids of his class had given Tones a rather, abusive type of nickname, 'Fatherless'

There was Emily, James, Trotter, Franklin, Ishudh, John, Racheal, Anne, Ed, Jim and Rottery in their class and I guarantee you none of them except for Ishudh, Tones and Trotter will be of use to this story.

Trotter was here, Tones was getting his desk set up for the day, "Howdy again, fella, fresh new day?" asked Trotter in a mood of excit, composed of evil however as per his expression of 'knuckle cracking' in a smouldering temper. "Whatever..." replied Tones is huffs and puffs indicating hatred towards him, most probable.

Trotter was about to start his tape record for the day but unfortunately for him though, the bell of the start had rung. Ishudh was Tones's best friend, he was the only person that Tones would share his all with since he had none-other and so that very day right after school was over, Tones sat of the stairs of the school stage with Ishudh and started to yab on all about the dream that he had had.

"The thing I WAS WEARING!..." he went on.."INSANE!"
"So what do you want to do about it, Tones it's just a dream..everyone...has a dream...once in a while" Ishudh said bringing an extremely awkward pause to the ongoing terrific conversation, but little did he know, that what he just said would alter something in little Tones's mind.

"It was my father that I saw, I've never seen him! Yet! I had such a fine and pristine image of him right next to me! SITTING!" Tones said, now, in a tone of debate.
"What exactly are you...Tones....trying to prove here...What exACtly?" asked Ishudh calmly back again.
"The fact that it was not JUST a dream but something more real than that and if so, how do I get back to it?" Tones yelled, quite aggressive at this point to be honest.
"You want to play that dream or whatever you call it AGAIN? It's not a youtube video, for context Tones..." said Ishudh in a manner quite professional.
"Look, brother...it's getting late and you don't want that hefty mum of yours to start jabbing about it...do you? I'll do some research on my side but please, get it off your mind!"
"Alright then..Thanks, just what I wanted!" said Tones, now chilled and satisfied and he was now on his way back home, with many hopes for the next day.

CHAPTER 04
I THINK THERE'S A WAY

"Yes, yes my dear, there's hope, within your friend it shall ly today! And from it shall you receive!" a glowing embrace of a golden palm Tones felt. The fingers of glowing glitter of love and sensation ran across Tones's cold face.

"Dad!" Tones whispered in dream state as he awoke, he looked around as to see where he was only to realise that had had one of those high level types of dreams. "Friend..OH ISHUDH!" Tones had a few adrenaline hormones rushing through his veins now.

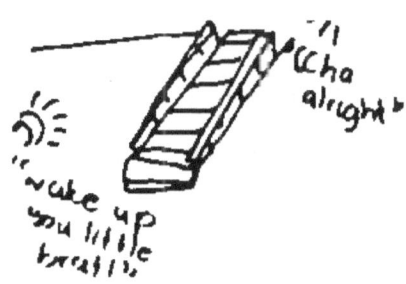

He was fast out of his bed, neither his mum's morning wake morn was to push his emotions down! He was in haste as it only took him seconds to finish off his morning starters and get dressed.

With a bye of no reply at all, he was off to school walking again, pretty usual at this point. "Midst Highway!" sighed

Tones as he ran in through the gate and right to his classroom only to be stopped by none other than Trotter himself.

"What up fella, couldn't catch ya yesterday! But I will make sure today!" he rang as one of those birds that came out of those vintage clocks whenever they gave off the hour pass alarm.

"Get out of the way! NOW! IM BUSSYY!" yelled Tones, losing his child and enthusiastic spirit for a second or 2 there. "You think I'd let you go, huh, looser, FATHERLESS!" re-rang the cuckoo clock as he held back Tones from his bag handle. "JUST..LETTT....ME......GO! GO!" he yelled and then with a humongous rush of strength he fled free from the scene.

A couple of children had started clapping their hands in chants of "fatherless" at Tones to which Tones had no effect at all. He was too absorbed to the idea of a 'real dream'. Ishudh was unloading his books to the desk tray.

"Oh-," he started.

"Yes...You FOUND IT RIGHT??!!" continued Tones.

"Firstly, Good morning, secondly yes, I think there's a way, you have to concentrate about it apparently, when you go to sleep, that is..." replied Ishudh. "Right, GOT IT!

Good Morning! Yes... I was being held up by Trotter along the corridor, you know.." said Tones, changing topics suddenly as to if he had now finally won his goal and was to have a rest.

"That cuckoo clock eh? HA! Don't care about him, he's just got something wrong in his mind, really, you're fine, alright?" said Ishudh with a really calming tone of immense care, which he indeed did bear to his lonely friend, Tones.

The first bell of the day had rung and on started their timetable, they rushed through it like a breeze and it was after that they started to have a proper chat at their usual place of school stage stairs.

Tones now took his time to start on about the dream that he had seen that very morning, "A dream JUST MAKES you THINK BUT THIS! I FELTTT—IT!". It turned out to be the theme and phrase of conversation and it would be an easy guess to say the person wo=ho made it so.

Tones was quite sceptical however, of the finding of Ishudh though he didn't really seem to overthink it.

"You sure right?" asked Tones quite exactly for the 6th time. "I won't tell you again, it's supernatural stuff we're talking, it's a try you take, not a guarantee"

"So I shall let you know tomorrow then! See Ya!"
"Yeah sure! Bye!" brought closure to the conversation.

CHAPTER 05
WHAT? IT IS?

The day at home was all rubbish as his 'so called Mum' had heard about Tone's talk of dreams at school. "You claim to see your dad, little brat?" she went on and Tones was having his evening shower. "So what, it's not as if you care!" argued Tones, the statement was so strong that Natalia had a pause to realise how mindful the child is.

"That WOMAN, anyways...I've got a dream to catch up!" Tones whispered to himself, extra knowledge, this was the 4th time he did so. This made dinner run quickly allowing bed time to swoop up fast and so was Tones's extreme impatience level.

"Concentration.....Concentration..." he started to remind himself. "Just remember the exact incident.." and with that he was no longer thinking, deep sleep had now engulfed him as he now had started to snore.

His brain however had other plans as the carving imprint of his 'father's dream' sprang back in. "Tones, my dear, welcome...welcome back!" Tones heard a familiar voice, a voice he had heard before. "Father? Is it———————you?"

was the first thing that came to his mind. Of course, he was in a mood of uncertainty and blur but his voice was clear enough to be understood, most fortunately.

"Yes..Yes..my child, It's me, Rud!" said the familiar person with a familiar voice. Tones's eyes were starting to regain its clear vision and then he came to the point where he could properly see.

A person was looking down at Tones with his eyes gleaming and the peacock feathers upon his head dangling down in love to the ground, most probable explanation eh?

"Hello!" said he, it was no doubt his father.

"DAD! OH MY GOD! IT WORKED!" Tones yelled(emphasise the 'yelled' while reading please) as concentration seemed to have worked, for obvious reasons. "Yes, IT HAS, I TOLD YOU! This very morning, right? Remember?" asked Rud, now that his extreme thrill too had spiced up by a ton. "Oh yes! I do! Whenever I sleep, now! I can JUST THINK OF YOU! AND I CAN

COME TO YOU!" Tones went on... "Yes, Good you know now!"

"So, I have a ton of questions..." started Tones, "You said I have to face a ton to get to that 'end point of imagination' right?" Tones went on with his first question which shall pave the path for more, many more. "Yes, your mind is the reason for all of this, it is the only thing able to surpass it, however, it will provide challenges based on experience and I guarantee you dear..It won't be easy!" replied Rud in a very serious mood, now that the questions seem to lead to somewhere quite not what a dad would want a child, more specifically his, to go through.

"You say it's not easy but I can, I definitely can! I JUST got to THINK about it and shall I be given the path," said Tones to Rud, who was getting more and more anxious with every word of the conversation. "You aren't going to try it are you?" he asked in release to some of his anxiety. "Most DEFINITELY! I-------------Will.." replied Tones, who seemed to know what his father was trying to get at but seemed to not care at all.

"Well------then.......indeed....am I concerned of your safety, however, it seems to be as if you are capable, I can help in ways but there is this one thing you must know..--" went on Rud.

"What...What is it?" asked Tones, jumping into the statement.

"It is that you shall face the reality of this!" replied Rud who seemed to give a sense of depression with it, and he went on, "The reality of Drong and Yeld and the life of Earth, you shall know my child."

CHAPTER 06
THE DAY HAS COME...

The night had already passed, "Friday," said Tones to himself, he was neither sad of his dream's end nor greedy for more time to it. He had managed to grasp all he'd need to voyage to his destination, more specifically, "the end point of imagination," said Tones as he rubbed his eyes and was up again for his day to day robotic routine.

He was quite excited to what he was to conquer and didn't seem to mind the immense amount of obstacles he'd have to drill through, yet, he went on with brushing his teeth to dressing up, all, calm and in a profound manner. You could tell his behavioural difference by the words of Natalia that very morning.

"What's gotten into you? That filthy 'dream' of yours is rotten you to the bone! Well, in fact, it's rotten to bone already BUT I'll see where this goes..."

"The fact that she's not in prison right now, bothers me about the social security that exists in this country!!" blabbered Tones to himself in disgust to his 'blah!'

Tones was now off to school, his shoes weren't ever as polished as much as that day, but however would get it dusty in no time. He was now in school, where sinister, hope, love all, clash together forming a muddy pulp of utter uselessness.

Tones ran to class to explain it all to Ishudh, who was amused ,quite surprisingly, at what Tones had said. "Where's Trotter?" asked Tones in a mood of scrutiny. "Don't know, why ask?" replied Ishudh. "It's just that he didn't seem to get to me today.....you think he's over heard us? Since you know..my mum knew about it all...and no one anywhere knows me well to hate me save for Trotter right?"

"Oh right yeah! Good thinking! Hmmm...Could be..."

The morning bell had rung and it was time for the friends to give a pause to their chat.

They however aced through the day with no problems, the funny part was how Trotter never seemed to come to school. It was when Ishudh and Tones were discussing, that this sprung into chat. "Trotter, probably might've heard how to get into a dream purposefully and he must be researching how to do so and attack!" Tones started to jab. "Hyperbole," replied Ishudh to the most superstitious like approach Tones had ever taken to him in his life. "If it is possible to get back into one, it should most likely be possible to get into another's one!"

Tones had ended the chat having both the pirates, Tones and Ishudh in 2 ideas, one being that one is able to sneak into another's dream which was supported by Tones and the other idea being that one CAN'T sneak into another's dream which as expected was supported by Ishudh.

Tones as he was returning home, however, had none of the power and agility that he had till then, but was rather anxious and nervous. "The day has come..." he started to think. "I must be able to conquer that field of mind power, if that is all that it takes to surpass the end point of imagination!" "That Trotter would come! I KNOW! I MUST! Be able to kick him back and achieve my goal!"

He was at home by no time and was getting ready for his so called 'mind battle' (Which his friend Ishudh took as stupidity) and he was ready by the set of the sun.

CHAPTER 07
THE GREAT REQUEST

"Get to bed!" rang Natalia, the only set of words which Tones seem to be needing now had arrived. He jumped onto his bed in his fresh new pyjamas. "I must be done with my mission by sunrise, somehow!" he determined to himself. He soon went asleep, deep sleep to be exact, with his concentration alongside him as the base towards the extreme journey he was to face.

He now heard the smooth rhythm of the to and fro ripples of tall waves, he was beside a tree on the cliff side of Nebulus. "Arggg!" said he as he rubbed his eyes with his cold fist in the shine of the hot sun. He got up, his suit serving to the uncomfiness. Rud wasn't to be seen. Tones was walking towards the town. The shepters house was busy on his left while the minors house on the right were gardening, well, not all of them that it... The gravel chip filled path was not of match to the tough leather soled shoes. Tones was engaging in travel which composed of a bit of run(when he felt energised) and a slow walk(when he started to get exhausted). He now was passing the area with the peakers, cattlers, and the other minors houses, the path now

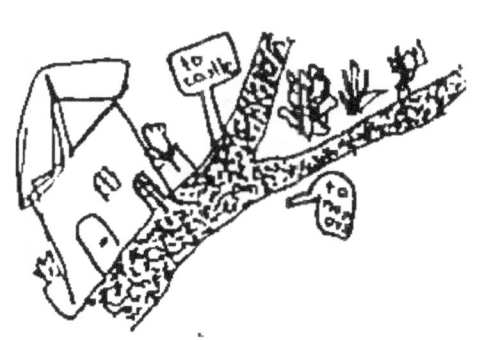

branched. One led to the castle, it seemed to be not much of a shabby one but a rather normal house looking building that was oversized.

 Tones had none other reason but to find his dad somehow, so he chose the path to the castle, where advice and probability resided.
The path was not of gravel chips but of a fine and thin layer of yellow sand. The sides of the path weren't the busy streets now but a beautifully arranged array of electron plants.

"Where is he? Hopefully here!" sighed Tones as he was walking, with an increase of fear on each step he took. His eyes moved all around his surroundings, the surroundings started to get colder and colder, the castle was near. Tones was sweating all this time but now it seemed to have been relieved.

The soldiers who were called Drocters were standing there, 2, on either side of the golden gates with an arch bridge like rod with the carvings of a cow, sheep, peacock as their appearance respectively and the word 'Yoda Goddess to Drong and Yeld' as well.

"Wow..." gasped Tones as he saw the castle with the Drocters, the colour theme of gold, yellow and black were all just clever! It looked majestic!

Tones went up to one of the Drocters, quite bravely, he went, "Vudyounomefater?" Nervousness seemed to strike back. "Pardon...?" asked the Drocter, most kindly, he was concerned. Tones took a quite unnecessary 5 second period of silence after which he regained consciousness of his presence near the Drocter and started, "Yes, my dad, Ruddey long for Rud..He is missing?"

"Oh good ol' Rud? Yeah! He is in the castle, you're his son I see.."

"Yes, Tones, his son...May I meet him?" asked Tones very childishly. "Yes, in you go now! Near the Palaka, be respectful" said the Drocter as he turned the gate behind his allowing entrance. Tones gave a nod par of smile and in he ran, his feathers gliding through the air.

The Palaka is more of the king, king to Drong and now that Tones had passed the entrance, he was now in walk rather than of run. His auditory senses started to kick in. "Lord, he shall face it!" "You and I can help!" "I believe in him!" "How?" "A child??!!" "SOME GET THE CHILD!" "You cannot possibly let a child...." It was a hot conversation, was the only thing Tones could think of. The sound was increasing, he was near...

Two Drocters were running towards him, in high speed, as if they were chased. "It's Tones! The kid! He's here! PHEWW!" rang one of the Drocters. Tones stood dead, he was on the fence. "Was I caught for trespassing or something? I've the gatekeeper's permission!" Tones was having his own miniature mental debate.

The Drocters took Tones close to them and went, "Listen boy, you better come, it's quite heck of you to do this type of things, reaching the end point? Really?" Tones resisted to reply and understood what they were onto, his dad had tried to ask the Palaka for permission... "Alright" sighed Tones as he walked into the head room, now with the company of the 2 Drocters.

"Child, m'dear, welcome! Palaka, it's me!" Your dad is he?.."

"Yes, that's right"

"And he claims that you claim to venture a journey most impossible?" the Palaka raised his hand which pointed towards the coastline.

"The end point? It is possible, and yes I have," replied Tones, with immense courage. The minister looked at Tones in suspicion. You see, the hall was spacious, red padded walls with golden inkings of mountains, just like on the end point of imagination. 6 ministers, 3 on either side sitting in chairs of velvet, green and blue with leather padded seats, while the Palaka sat on the chair made of thick gold with black, refine leather for the back and seat.

"Well then, Rud," Palaka took a depressed look at Rud, who seemed begish. "It's proven but let me know, if you've changed minds..." "But!" started the ministers on the left who looked more of thin wine bottles with evil faces. "No more questions!"

Tones and Rud took a look at each other smiling in a heavenly look. Tones woke up.

CHAPTER 08
ALL IS SET!

"Well, I guess it's postponed then..." Tones whispered to himself as he got off bed. Tones's natural alarm system, his mum, Natalia, was ringing quite loudly at the time. "Wait a second...why? IT'S A SATURDAY!" yelled back Tones, quite justified as it was not a school day.

"Somebody is here, you friend it seems, best?" Natalia had soon turned into an innocent piece of human flesh. As to why you may ask? Probably because a guest is over? Yes! Congrats! You are right!

Tones knew at that moment, who had come, he had none-other to be friends with but Ishudh. It was most definitely him, Tones was quite thrilled now. "Coming then!" A tune of joy played in the back of his mind.

Tones rushed down, having Natalia questioned on whether Tones was actually in state of sleep a few minutes ago.

"Hey!" waved Tones.

"Hi!" said Ishudh as he walked in embracing the warmthness of an un-home like home. They both walked into Tones's room, not giving care towards Natalia, who tried to make company in rubbish of a way. Tones now had again started to jabber about his favourite topic, the dream!

"My favourite animal is the best part, they've got it everywhere, just now did I realise it!" continued Tones.

"Say, what is your most favourite animal?" asked Ishudh quite in a way that an FBI officer would have questioned.

"The peacock!" replied Tones enthusiastically. "Woh, I see,...nice..." responded Ishudh trying to be normal but it seemed as if he hid something.

"So like today is the day, I face it all!" ended Tones.m "The start of all Tones, and soo.....wanna watch a movie for, I dunno practice?" "Ohhh, brain practice eh? Good point, let's do an adventure one!" replied Tones, as he sat on the bed in front of his computer. The computer, most fortunately, had a large enough screen which was enough for the 2 to view at a distance and so they loaded a movie. A movie of pirates fighting against a vast ocean of sea monsters to get to a land of treasure having his own foes on his back.

It served of some importance to Tones as his mind was learning 'tactics' apparently to face his adventure to the so-called 'end point of imagination'. Tones had watched it before but never seemed to have cared for the tactics but now he did.

The movie came to an end as both of them had a chit chat about how cool Francis, jumped across an entire boat, holding his son whilst taking down an entire dozen other foe pirates. Tones had a much more broader view of the matter however as he had, for obvious reasons, watched it before.

"No way! That wasn't his son!?" questioned Ishudh, well surprised at Tones's knowledge. "Yeah, it was all an easter egg..."

Time passed like wind and soon the 2 friends found themselves in a situation of departion. "Alright mum! Well, then good luck Tones!" Ishudh waved bye to Tones. "Oh yeah, and I know Trotter will be there!" replied Tones in a serious mood. The two had had a bit of an argument on whether 'dream trespass' was even a thing.

In a nutshell, Tones was super natural while Ishudh kept himself to logic and science.

CHAPTER 09
A BIG MISSION OF DREAM STARTS

"You need some sort of object to get through Yeld," said Buklow, a friend of Rud, close. "A ship? All you need is a ship..." replied Tones, seeming astoundingly well knowledgeable. "Wadyu, mean 'ship'?" asked Buklow holding his eucalyptus juice mug in his right. "Well, it's a 'human' thing, can voyage over water without a sink now!" interrupted Rud, who was clarified by Tones's well nod.

"So the question is how to get one of it..." came back Buklow with a strong argument, he continued, "It's just me and Tones on the journey, you better find a good one of those ship things..."

"Wait so dad isn't coming?" sprang Tones, who was then replied by Rud and Buklow respectively.. "No, my child, it is said, the one to venture is to be alone unless another joins midway, I can only appear mentally and provide support by mental means!" "Your dad's alright, I too would abandon you on your way, alone is alone...." Tones showed signs of disbelief and give-up but then seemed to self motivate himself as he replied, "All fine, then..." "Sheep?"

asked Buklow. "Huh? It's Ship "i"," corrected Rud. "If mind power can reach an endpoint and pass through it, why can't it build a thing?" questioned Tones as if Issac Newton were to question the apple on why it fell down instead of going up.

"I call that clever!" clicked Buklow, with an innocent smile upon his face as he looked back at Rud, who showed no sign of excite but rather an expression of seriousness and what-even-do-you-mean.

"Well...do it...take it as a warm up to strengthen-----your

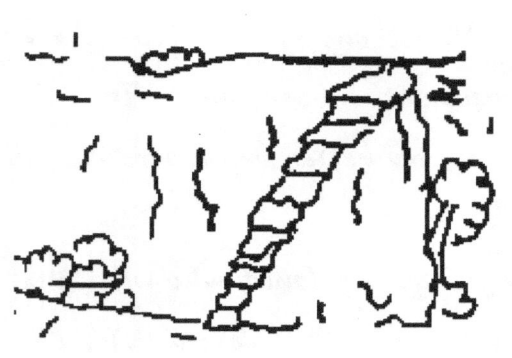

mind, get on the beach," sighed Rud who then pointed at a set of stairs, carved on munched boulders that slid off the slope of the seaside cliff.

They slowly and with most care climbed the stairs down. They were very much worn away, each step was an accomplishment of 'not-dying'.

Soon enough however, they were on the warm beach, the sun was close to the mountains on the edge, it was the evening. "Alright, then, think about it and THINK about it, each single ray of detail of it and place your focus on the location you need it at..." said Rud as he bent down towards Tones's face, desperately hoping he won't mess up bad.

Tones focused on the waters of Yeld, Buklow was staring intensely at the intense stare. An unexpected, abnormal ripple shook the surface of the water which Tones was looking at. "Ar———————————ghh—hhhhh——-hhh!" gave up Tones, who seemed to succeed in level 01.

"Alright, that was cool, come on, try again..." reassured Buklow, with his long yellow beard swinging in the wind and his face long and round like a chinese fellow. Rud kept in his mood of intensity. Tone retried, the splashes went higher this time, however it wasn't a success.

"What's pushing you back?" questioned Rud, now fully embedded into the situation. "Mind's changing ideas dad..."

"The hidden god Yudanti, God to evil and disruption, don't let her get to you!" "Focus kid!" Tones gave an okay-got-it nod to both Rud and Buklow and tried back at it again. The splashes were now as if something hard banged on it, wood was slightly visible, translucent however. They all disappeared!

"ARR!" cries of shivering echoed out the waters. "The Yeldians!" alarmed Buklow. "It's not of care for now, Tones focus...." rang Rud, starting to turn a bit aggressive at this point to be honest.

Tones took at look at the crying waters, "Yoda, Goddess to Yeld and Drong, allow me, allow me to conquer this field of mind power!", the thud was now completely visible as rings of water splashed round, wood nailed itself as nails sprang into position. The sails were raised with inkings of 'Francis's Love' on it. A head of a chinese dragon was carved at the head of the ship.

Something of a twinkle ringed on the ship's main level, but it didn't seem to catch the attention of the 3.

The cries of the Yeldians, turned to screeches and faded away to silence all of a sudden. Tones was staring dumbfounded on

What he had just done. Buklow gave a kind clap of appreciation, while Rud sprung into

his classical heavenly smile, part of the mission had been now completed successfully.

CHAPTER 10
PREPARE OF BATTLE

"That's it! WAKE UP! 25TH TIME!" Natalia yelled grasping Tones by the shoulders and shaking him to life from a sleepy state. "Ah! FINE! MOVE!" yelled back Tones in extreme hate and annoyance. "Again! NO SCHOOL!" Tones continued his attitude.

Natalia pulled the clock which hung on the wall in front Tones's bed and she held its face to Tones's face. "HERE!" she added. Tones, not caring at all, observed the patterns that ran round the clock, he hadn't seen them before. 'Intecto Saturi Meo Do Nos' it said. Tones showed a sign of smile.

"Funny, you find it?! IT'S 11:30! YOU BETTER EAT YOUR BREAKFAST NOW! IT'S COLD BUT I DON'T CARE!" re-added Natalia in her mood of distress. Tones came to the sudden realisation on what his mum was on about and showed sign of defeat within their miniature argument.

"Alright...Alright..." sighed Tones as he woke up and went to have his breakfast, leaving Natalia in a smouldering temper. Tones was left thinking of emptiness after breakfast, as he had nothing at all to do.

His brain suddenly was reminded of his so-called 'mission'. "I could just plan it couldn't I?" So Tones, now, having nothing at all to do, went up, back to his bedroom, in order to jot down and plan his way of battle.

"So my only foes shall be the Yeldians and that Trotter, Trotter should be easy to push off and well, the Yeldians would quite obviously be the tough ones, I've just NEVER SEEN EM!" "I could just SLEEP NOW! Which is impossible since i'd slept for soo long! OH THINK!" "I bet the Yeldians would show much resemblance to sea monsters, like in those films, deadly, creepy and vicious! Well, their voice says it all!"

Fortunately there was his father's little box which had all sorts of things that seem to link to Tones's dream world. Pictures of peacocks, cattle and sheep, his father was a geologist, photographer. "Only if father was here..." sighed Tones as he moved his fingers over the dusty old pictures.

Tones moved some away to delve a bit deeper into the box, to see the words, words which he had never come across in that very box. The very words which he had seen that very day upon the edge of his room clock, 'Intecto Saturi

Meo Dos Nos'. A yellow tinted paper was it, Tones with extreme curiosity pulled it out and unfolded the paper more which was a couple years old now. It read,

'INTECTO SATURI MEO DOS NOS' **meaning Love to Lord, My God he is, was found carved on a 20, 000 year old stone.**

It was from a cut off newspaper, the nature of the piece of paper said so. Tones took a look at the top edge of the old paper, it confirmed his assumptions.

"It's from the Times.." said Tones to himself. "How come have I not spotted this before, could it possibly link to my dream? IMPOSSIBLE!" Tones kept his eyes on the paper

for a few seconds and then scavenged his father's box again.

He pulled past the listings of 'ancient plants, good luck?' as he had read it before, to find nothing new. "I guess that's it....hmph..." whispered Tones, the fellow boy getting lazy ever second he kept the next few hours walking round the neighbourhood appreciating the little details of plants, trees and cracks on the road. The evening however soon came to an end.

Later however, in accords to his strategy of 'More tire More sleep' he successfully got himself tired, had dinner pretty early and went to bed early, again.

A question, however, stood out that kept Tones nervous throughout the time and that was if the dream was pausable? Sure you could stop it and come back later but what about the timeline, would it stay paused or would it just restart or would it just go on...and if it did restart, what would happen if such a break happens mid-way in the mission, WOULD HE HAVE TO START AGAIN!!??

CHAPTER 11
LET THE BATTLE BEGIN

Tones was looking at the ship with the sun gleaming upon it just as it did before. The heavenly smile state Rud was still in and the amazed state of Buklow were both still intact. Time hadn't passed. Tones lept into laughter, he didn't mention the time pause but continued his laughter. "M'child, you DID IT!" "Told you! You just the best!" Rud hugged Tones tight and wept bitterly. "From here shall I depart...Buklow shall lead you halve way and it'll just be you!" "Alright dad, I won't let you down!" replied Tones in a warmth of courage and helpfulness. This brought some sort of a strong feeling within Rud as he whipped off his tears with his sweaty hands of fear and anxiousness.

Tones now, with a wave of a goodbye that may or may not be good, walked over the golden sand in his shoes as every step meant to being closer to danger, Tones got onto the ship. Buklow slowly climbed up and oh was he over the moon! "I'm UPON YELD!" he yelled joyously. Tones, being the only one on board who seemed to know 'ships', grasped the wheel which was fresh as if it were cut off from a tree a day before. Buklow, stubbed his feet over the main lay in curiosity of sink. With a last look at Rud, Tones was ready.

The sails unfolded themselves in magic of a movement and the silent, yet cold wind pushed the ship along the shiny waters and towards the end, they sailed.

"Hmm—ph—hhhhh---, get ready boy, another 50 metres and I'll leave ya!" Buklow said all of a sudden. "Right...." exclaimed Tones in mood of 'aware'. The metres soon passed without a wait and it was time of departure for the 2. The sun was to set as the horizon gleamed in a tint of yellow and red, Buklow disappeared without a word...

"This is it...just me----------------------alone........"

A SCREECH!
A YELL!
A SCREAM!
A LAUGH!

All from everywhere, the limits of Drong were passed and he was in another's land. "Yeld......" whispered Tones as he scavenged 360 degrees round him in search

for danger. A sound was detected by Tones, it was from the lower floor of the ship, thuds of footsteps they were, it was getting louder
and was it shiverish. It was now to the point where it made Tones's hair stand on end and both his hands widened apart in mood of attack.

"You know me..."

"I have come..."

"A filthy little dream of yours"

"You and your stupid mission"

It was all a familiar voice, till he revealed himself and it was none other than the Trotter boy, "Trotter, it's you huh?" replied Tones back to the voice. Out the stair hole he erupted as a fat, freckled boy with dark black hair...Tones was well in mood to strike now.

The screams still ECHOED....It wasn't by Trotter now. A loud thud by the south of the ship. Trotter who was about to train towards Tones, turned back. Tones and Trotter both were alarmed and they were sweating, indeed, in anxiety.

Tones, who knew it was the Yeldians, kept his mouth shut, Trotter however yelled out cluelessly. "Who's that??!! SHOW your FACE! Tones's army??!!" 3 fingers, with patches of moss all over them, sharp and with long nails they were, a hand grasped the edge of the ship. It dripped with water, "Trotter... move back..............it's...........it's not what you expect..... Just trust me!" Tones tried to warn Trotter but he seemed to have other things in mind. "OH... COME ON!"" Trotter kept himself

to misconduct. "Raaaaaaaaa! YELDDDDD!" screeched the hand. A large scaled monster of sea, sharp, black canine teeth, with a hard boned body and toes of knives, jumped on the ship board.

It-------------was-----terrifying----. It had a tail of shark

and no neck. "Holy...." jinxed both Trotter and Tones. Tones kept focus however but Trotter was, you guessed it!, running for his life! The monster was on focus of his simple-to-him movements of Trotter which seemed to have alarmed it as it,

"RAAAA!!!! THIS!!!!! MY LANDDDDD!!!!!!!!!" reverberated the monster in a ghost like horrifying voice.
The sound seemed to have invited other fellow sea monsters as the poor Trotter, out of his wits, was hiding behind a barrel when a large watery and slimy like octopus tentacle smothered round his like a python!
"AHH—-RRRRhhhHHH-HHHHHHH" Trotter kept yelling but the Yeldians seemed to have no mercy. Trotter was pulled to the sky as if it was a film while Tones kept himself to spectator mode.

He was pulled into sea, and was no more to be seen. "Oh...my...god..." Tones said feverishly as his heart pounded against him. The ship was receiving all sorts of attacks all around. The shark monster who had been staring yet, glided towards Tones.
"NOOOOOOOOOOOOOOOOOOO!" CRIED TONES!
SLICE!   CHING!   SLAY!

"Francis?" Tones said confusingly as he suddenly seemed to have forgotten what was going on. The creature laid dead, in pieces of 3 or 4 on the floor millimetres away from Tones. It was indeed Francis, Francis from the movie. A pirate he was... "Move back boy, here's a sword, use it wisely, and now........ Let's beat THESE ONES UP!" he started in heroic of a tone.

Francis went towards the octi monster who had already grasped the ship making it unable to move. Tones and Francis both ran towards the tentacles. Francis, who was ofcourse well experienced, sliced the tentacles one shot. Blood or gue of slimy green leaked out the bodies. It took Tones a well over 3 smacks to slice off a tentacle, which seems worse at first but if you delve deeper to the fact you will be able to understand that torture is wayyyy worse than 1 shot and therefore Tones was the better fighter though he was just a child at the age of 6. "TONES EAST!" a loud yell from Francis. A large snake of

fierce, slithered among the ship top board near the steering wheel. Tones dodged many of its

venomous strikes. The snake Jumped over as Tones crept under in sweat of fear and he stabbed the snake as hard as he could, blood leaked away in tons of amounts and the snake seemed to loose strength. It still continued however, weaker, it slithered into cobra formation with Tones in front and rushed its head towards Tones with its mouth wide open. Tones quite wisely sliced through the inner mouth of the snake and BANG! Dropped the snake in a soul of no life.
The thuds and screeches were no more!
Francis had taken down a dozen other shark monsters and 2 octis alongside another snake and they both quite obviously were exhausted.
"We won right?" gasped Tones.

CHAPTER 12
REACHES A LAND OF TREASURE

Tones woke up quick, his mum wasn't calling him, he was so happy that he succeeded in level 2 of the mission that his adrenaline made him awake. "The dream is pausable, nothing to worry...phew..." he said to himself in thrill of a mood.

He got off doing his morning activities as it was school day and he went down for breakfast. The fresh yet uncooked and not-at-all-delicious.....its....not pasta? It was noodles this time for Tones and he was more than grateful. "Boy you acting good today, hiding something?" Natalia asked quite surprised and kindly.

Tones kept quiet and soon enough, Tones was at school, no sweat drop of fatigue did he have, a mind of purity was it. He ran through the corridor. Trotter was there...perfectly fine... He didn't seem to come on to Tones either! He nor was welcoming...and just like a stranger he went. "Probably afraid of me now! Ha!" Tones whispered to himself having a bit of courage running through his veins.

Ishudh was by his desk and he waved. "How'd it go?" he asked abruptly. "Good morning! Yes! It went GREAT!" Tones then went on explaining Francis and Trotter, the fact that Trotter was suffocated and the amazing intro of Francis and his way of attacks.

"Hmmm.....I see...." replied Ishudh, again, hiding something which Tones didn't seem to take note of. "So today, if possible, I must reach the end point...." said Tones. "You know what happens next?" asked Ishudh with a glitter of suspicion. "Dunno..." replied Tones, still thrilled. "Welp, most 'hidden' places, have a puzzle to get through, so yeah! Could---------could----be a puzzle..." Ishudh sent his eye balls round the scene.

"Oh yeah! Good point!" stated Tones.

School time was spent normal, Tones learnt about the 'hierarchy of needs' which seemed really interesting to him.

Tones was back home, he finished his homework and had lunch and then dinner. He was setting up his bed to get through 'level 3' done. His mum, Natalia, didn't seem to be much troublesome at all that day and Tones very much appreciated it.

The night approached and Tones slept without a word between his mother.

"Boi, you better be grateful for that save!" exclaimed Francis, wrapping his arm round Tones. Tones having just entered the dream world, was weak. "Yeah....close...call...quarantee..." he replied. Francis was in mood of energy, Tones, on the other hand, was finding yuck to see the bleeding fins of the shark monster, he yet made sure to stare at it. It was spitting out goo, which smelled horrible. "How are you-----here! Like------here!" Tones asked Francis abruptly in face of extreme confusion.

"Long story, I was sleeping.....but anyways.......we've got more stuff to worry about don't we?"

"Yes, Yes.......you're right.." gasped Tones as he went towards the top board of the ship observing the darkness engulfing the feverishly yellow sky. The mountains on the endpoint were now bigger.

The stars were gleaming brightly as the moon fought for the position of sun. Tones felt something, a glitch, everything round him started to disappear and re-appear. His visuals were breaking apart uncontrollably, the endpoint was getting nearer and nearer. "ARRGGGG! TONES!!!! THINK!!!" yelled out Francis in agony and pain. A rush of warm blood circulated round Tones as he fell down on his knees. Fatigue and dreaminess was crippling round him and Francis was now screaming louder than ever in extreme uncontrollability.

"DAD, APPEAR! HELP ME!" Tones yelled!

Screamed!

Reverberated!

Yelled!

TILL HIS LUNGS TORE APART!

A face....a cold face...of hope.....appeared. Rud was afraid, he was anxious as he stared at Tones.

"DEAR! THINK! CREATE A WORLD!!! THIS IS!!!!!!!!!!!! THE END!!!!" Rud yelled creating hope, he then glitched out, all sounds now tore apart to frequencies which cannot be explained.

Tones thought, a wonder land of what

he wanted, a puzzle his friend had warned about. The moon now tore apart, pain and

Agony, negativity engulfed him like a forcefully tied knot round his neck!

Francis laid dead as his colour faded away......Tones kept thinking,

He kept thinking,

He kept thinking,

He still went on...................

The sounds started to restore, the mountains disappeared, pain reverted to hope, Francis and Tones both were provided with relief. The ship beneath them burst as the night sky gleamed back to existence. Rays of rainbow scattered away in the explosion, Tones and Francis flew across the white dotted sky in an angelic move. They both held hands, "I DUNNO, WHAT'S THIS!!" questioned Francis, Tones kept observing with his smile growing with every turn he took. Behind them, the mountains which were the barrier till then, melted away to nothingness.

BAM!!!!

THUD!!!

Tones and Francis were smacked onto a new land, it was

all lush greenery round him, but it wasn't as green as it was supposed to be considering the fact it was night time, the reason was obvious.

"Woh? So like....I did it?" Tones huffed in exhaust as he saw Francis gasping for breath.

CHAPTER 13
A PUZZLE OF LOVE

"We better get, moving in, from my experience..." puffed Francis. "Alright, let's move...." The island was familiar to Francis, it was his treasure island. Tones and Francis both knew this at the time but never mentioned it to each other as they were too much soaked into the situation and the mission.

"Straight, and to the left from the 'x' carved tree alright?" questioned Tones in haste.

The forest covering grew larger and larger with every step they both took. "Faster, the gateway is near! Come on!" encouraged Francis to the little boy who was now failing to keep up.

The cold breeze rubbed amongst their wet and hardened skins of pain and obstacle.

Rust conquered the metal armours they wore and the feathers which had once beautifully been upon the hats were now left on in bits. Their leather shoe soles beaten down to a millimetre of thickness. They kept on running. Weak yet alarm setting sounds echoed around them. It was Francis's words that kept them going.
"COME ON!"
"BIT MORE!"
"STRAIGHT STRAIGHT!!!"
"RIGHT!"
"GO! GO!"
And they were there, a large and tall, ancient looking gateway. "This isn't the gate.......It's changed! NOOOO!" Tones and Francis both jinxed in fear as they both got confused. They were nervous and heartbroken yet Tones in spark of hope examined the gateway up close as Francis sat on the grassy soil. "There could and must be some kind of marking.....a clue?"

Carvings of a heart and money on either side with cracks all over and a cross looking crack in between. "Pick the right one?" interrupted Francis as he got up now in hope. "It must be some kind of such but if soo..." went on Tones but his sentence was then completed by Francis. "What could be the right one?" "It must be money!" exclaimed Francis, gold is everything a person could ask for, it makes you rich and successful.

"But love?" argued Tones, "Without it...would gold be useful....if you have none to share your FEELINGS WITH and if you have none to speak with and-------and--------"

"So you say love and I say money?" Francis came in... "How about we make a deal, I say mine first and let's see what happens?" Tones provided a solution. "If it didn't work?" asked Francis. "Well, then I'll be punished by the puzzle won't I?" replied Tones.

"LOVE OR MONEY, LOVE IT IS!" screamed Tones in face of courage and hope. It worked....The heart gleamed in shades of gold and pink of an outline. The moon turned to sun and the dark sky became blue as the trees sprung to its true colour. The wall now broke apart.

A shining and lava coloured, Goddess like figure appeared. She gleam in beauty and a glowing Goddess she really was. "Woh!" Tones and Francis both stuttered as they both took a step back.

"I"
"AM"
"YODA"
"GODDESS TO DRONG AND YELD"

Tones was shivering, no words came out his mouth, he continued to listen. "You my child, you------traveller-----have successfully surpassed the end point successfully, a task which none other had succeeded. LOVE is indeed GREATER THAN MONEY OR WEALTH" She went on in a smile as she bowed down and bowed both Tones's and Francis's head as if they were newborns. She then disappeared leaving the wall to crumble away revealing the world that they deserve. "WAIT!" Tones jumped, but no, she had already gone...

CHAPTER 14
THE END IS ALWAYS HAPPY AND SHORT

Tones wept happily as Francis came towards him and hugged him... "You were right....were right....child..." he whispered to Tones's ear and a bit away from them, Rud and Buklow appeared. "You did it!" Buklow yelled and Rud came upto Tones and cried as he hugged him happily. "M'child did it!" screamed Rud.

"Oh wow! Yes.." Tones whispered calmly as he still couldn't process the information on what was going on! Tones looked at Buklow who looked back at him in a heavenly smile. Keep in mind that Rud and Francis both were hugging Tones tightly, another one to hug could cause suffocation. Rud never seemed to have noticed however.

"OH BRING IT ON BUK!" yelled Rud in excite as all four hugged each other in a sphere of a form.

They ran through the wall to be greeted by a world which man would have all he'd ask for. Land of natural beauty with waterfalls, rivers and lakes, with flowers all round. The sun shined brightly and proudly in the sky enchanting the beautiful world below. Oh and there were piles of gold here and there, so they indeed had received money, and love! His father and of course Buklow... :)

Tones took a happy look at the majestic sight, which he had accomplished.

"I"

"DID"

"IT!"

"Wakey, Wakey BOI!" Natalia yelled, he was back, with his mission completed. Tones opened his glitter filled eye. "We both woke late!" "NO SCHOOL, GOOD SKIPPING METHOD OF YOU NOW.." shouted Natalia. All that Tones knew was that he had achieved something in his life and was now on to get on with it for more adventures...

The End!

"The fact that it was not JUST a dream..."

❊ ~**Tones**

"DEAR! THINK! CREATE A WORLD!!!..."
~Ruddey
Father of Tones ❊

Which one is the actual dream?
    Is it really a dream of sleep?
Or is it a new world.....?
    Will Tones succeed in his mission?
How can a dream be real?
    There has to be some reason!

Join Tones's adventurous world of reality and dream!

❊❊❊❊❊❊❊❊❊❊❊❊❊

www.ingramcontent.com/pod-product-compliance
Lightning Source LLC
LaVergne TN
LVHW041633070526
838199LV00052B/3330